THROUGH THE LENS

Of A

TEENAGE

SHARECROPPER

Dr. Gwen Sturrup Coverson

THE MOTIVATION AND IMPETUS
FOR WRITING THIS BOOK
IS DEDICATED TO
MY GREAT-GRANDMOTHER
ELLA LEWIS
WHO MADE IT POSSIBLE FOR
ME TO EXPERIENCE WORKING
AS A SHARECROPPER.

Published in the United States of America

ISBN 978-1-962569-04-0 (SC)
ISBN 978-1-962569-02-6 (HC)
ISBN 978-1-962569-03-3 (Ebook)

Gwendolyn Coverson Publishing
222 West 6th Street
Suite 400, San Pedro, CA, 90731
www.stellarliterary.com

Ordering Information and Rights Permission:

Quantity sales. Special discounts might be available on quantity purchases by corporations, associations, and others. For details, contact the publisher at the address above.

For Book Rights Adaptation and other Rights Permission. Call us at toll-free 1-888-945-8513 or send us an email at admin@stellarliterary.com.

THROUGH THE LENS

of a

TEENAGE SHARECROPPER

DR. GWEN S. COVERSON

Illustrated by Noble Sissle, III

Letter of Acknowledgement

I wish to express my sincere gratitude to Professor Noble Sissle, III of Florida A&M University who offered Invaluable assistance, support and guidance in the compilation of my book *"**Through the Lens of a Teenage Sharecropper**"*.

Our conversations and collaboration throughout this process inspired and motivated me to complete my book. Looking forward to many future endeavors and projects.

With Warm regards,

Dr. Gwen S. Coverson

RAILWAYS
BUS
42303

It was a sunny beautiful day when grandpa drove granny Ella and I to the ***Trailaway* Bus Station** in **Overtown** in Miami, Florida. **Overtown** is an African-American community where black folks settled around 1896. We checked our luggage, waved good-bye to grandpa, and boarded the bus. At 12 years old, I was leaving the state of Florida for the first time en-route to Doerun, Georgia. I was so excited because my granny had invited me to travel with her to meet my family in Georgia. To be honest, I think, I was the only one of my siblings who would go with her.

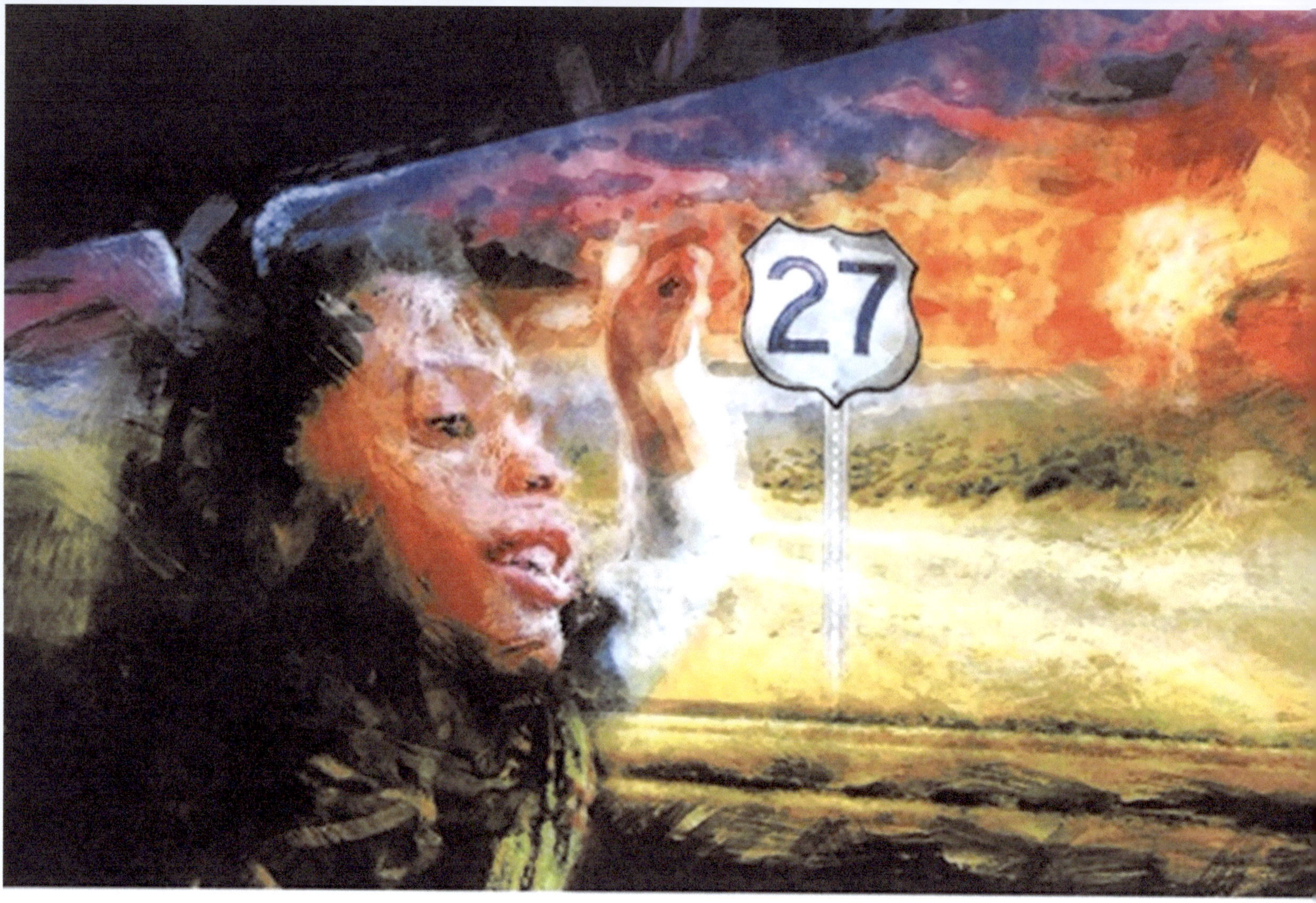
27

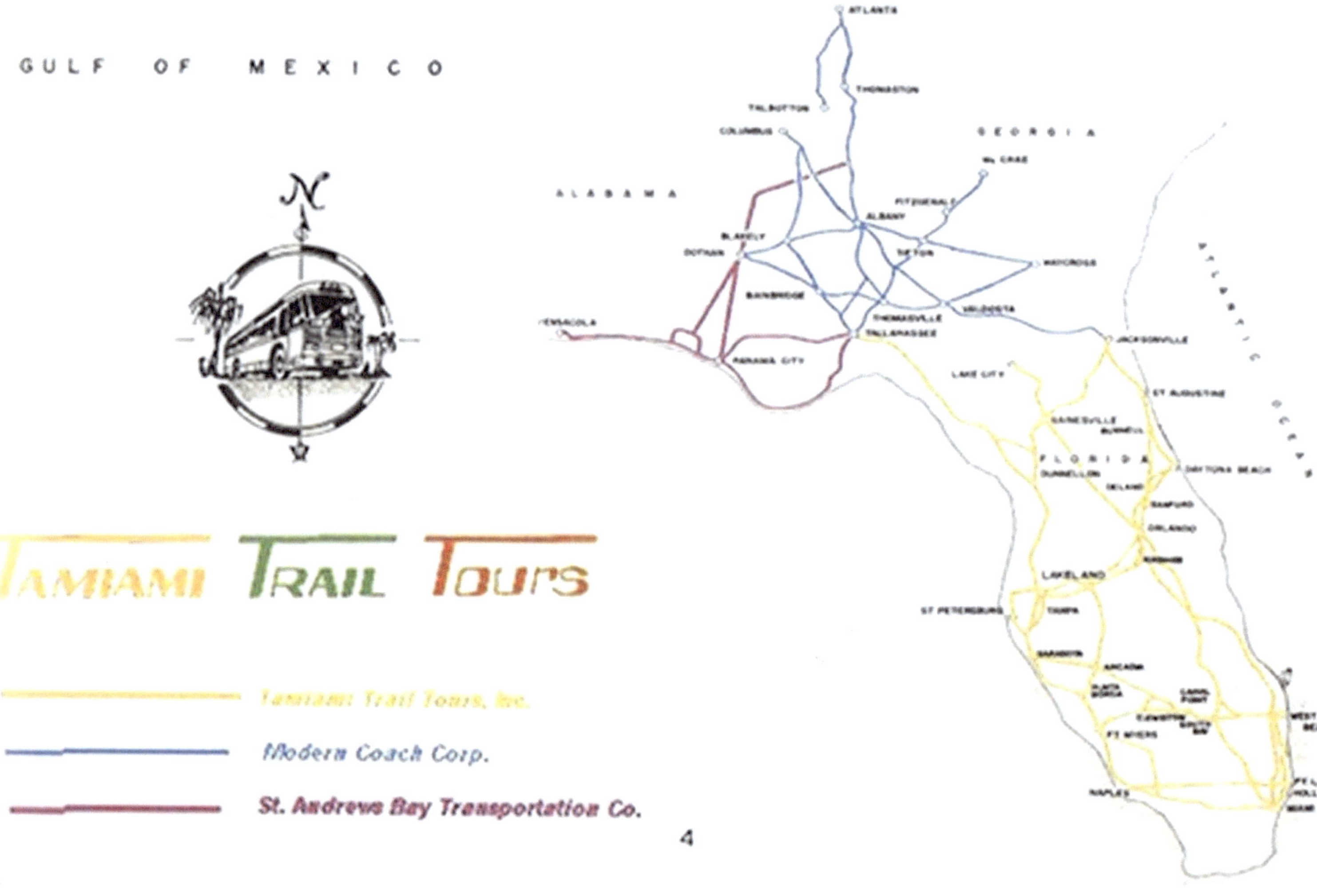
GULF OF MEXICO
ALABAMA
GEORGIA
FLORIDA
ATLANTA
THOMASTON
TALBOTTON
COLUMBUS
ALBANY
TIFTON
WAYCROSS
DOTHAN
BAINBRIDGE
VALDOSTA
THOMASVILLE
TALLAHASSEE
PENSACOLA
PANAMA CITY
JACKSONVILLE
LAKE CITY
ST AUGUSTINE
GAINESVILLE
DAYTONA BEACH
DUNNELLON
DELAND
SANFORD
ORLANDO
LAKELAND
ST PETERSBURG
TAMPA
SARASOTA
ARCADIA
FT MYERS
WEST PALM BEACH
NAPLES
HOLLYWOOD
TAMIAMI TRAIL TOURS
Tamiami Trail Tours, Inc.
Modern Coach Corp.
St. Andrews Bay Transportation Co.

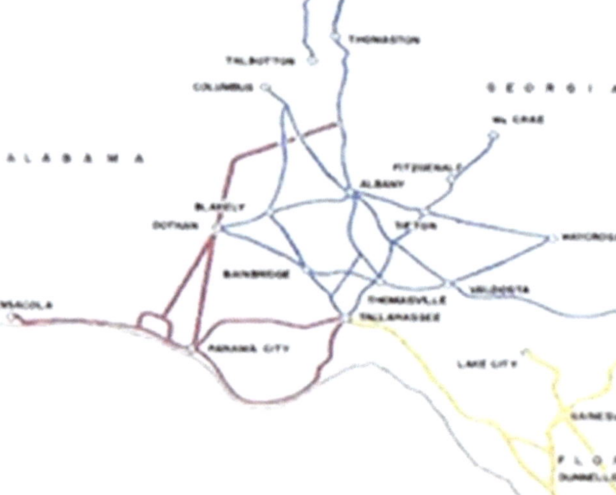

As we traveled on the bus, I enjoyed being with my granny Ella but the ride to Tallahassee was long and tiring. The countryside was beautiful. For miles and miles, we saw orange groves, cattle and palm trees. Granny and I took many naps along the *way*. My favorite time during the bus ride was eating the lunch my grandma Essie prepared for us. I will always remember those brown paper bags filled with fried chicken, pound cake and Coca-Cola sodas. As we finished our meal the aroma from the food was still in the air. All of a sudden, our eyes closed and we fell asleep.

We changed buses in Tallahassee (Capital of Florida), and soon thereafter arrived in Moultrie, Georgia. While waiting at the bus station, I asked granny why was there white and colored restrooms and see replied, "That's the way it is". At that moment and being a pre-teen, I did not realize I was a part of the Jim Crow Era which Encouraged segregation. This was a time when white folks and black folks shared separate facilities. Soon my cousin entered the bus station and was elated to see her Aunt Ella and me.

Once we arrived in Doerun, Georgia (country part of Moultrie) the entire family was there to greet granny and I. Even though this was my first time meeting them, I felt like I had known and loved them all my life. The house we lived in was owned by a Caucasian man named Mr. Smith. During post- reconstruction many families worked the land in exchange for a place to stay. Black farmers who did not own property would work a plot of land that was owned by white landowners. The black farmers would receive a share of the harvest and a place to stay as payment.

As a teenager, I was enthused about being around family. There were at least 20 relatives living in the same house, which seemed normal to me. Every morning around 5 am, we woke up to the smell of breakfast which was prepared by my aunt. She cooked smoked bacon, home-made biscuits with syrup and sweet tea.

Before breakfast we would use a large bowl filled with water to wash our faces and brush our teeth. There was no indoor plumbing therefore, we used a steel circular tub filled with water to wash our bodies. Outside adjacent to the house was the ***outhouse***, which was used as a restroom. An outhouse is an outside toilet enclosed by a wooden shed. Next to the outhouse was the ***hog pen***. While using the outhouse, you could hear loud noises and bad odors coming from the hog pen. After breakfast, everyone in the household would either work in the field or in town.

Soon we would hear a horn blow repeatedly, that meant it was time for us to load the truck and go to work in the fields. We would travel down a winding and bumpy road.

Throughout the week, I would go to various field locations. On Monday, we would pick peas. Tuesday's, we would pick peanuts. Wednesday's we would shake and stack tobacco. On Thursday's we would pick okra and Friday's we would gather and load watermelons on the back of a large trailer truck. We worked very hard all week. When we got thirsty during the day, we would fill our jars with clear spring water and drank it because spring water was clean and tasted better than well water. Well water was sometimes discolored and tasted bitter. We would work from sunrise to sunset. The days were extremely long end blazingly hot.

During the 1960's, the premier job for the older female adults were working in the big house (plantation style home) for the landlord. Some of the chores were cooking, washing, cleaning, ironing, shopping, etc. Although some of the younger adults worked in the city of Moultrie, Georgia, most of the young teenagers worked in the fields at least 12 hours per day.

Every Saturday our work shift would end at noon. We would form a straight line and the master would face us with envelopes filled with our pay. If the master felt you played around or goofed off while working he would deduct money from your pay. On occasion, my cousin would get his pay shorten because during the week the master would catch him playing instead of working. Soon the truck would arrive to take all the workers home. I would always give my great-grandmother half of my earnings which amounted to about $60.00 per week.

MOULTRIE

After work on Saturday afternoon, the family spent the remainder of the day playing checkers on the front porch, fishing, cooking, shopping or simply relaxing. My favorite past time was crossing the railroad tracks in downtown Moultrie to go shopping and to the movies with my cousins. We had so much fun.

Sunday was the most festive day of the week. After church, family members would gather at the house for dinner. My uncle would always pray before we ate. My favorite dish on the menu was home-made blueberry pie made with fresh blueberries. We would end the evening sharing family stories and playing checkers on the front porch.

OULTRIE

The summer had finally come to an end and it was time for granny and I to travel home. Early that morning, the family gathered on the front porch. We gave each other hugs, kisses and said goodbye. The summer became a lifelong memory. One of those lifelong memories, I want to share with the world.

THEN 1960's
VINTAGE
WELL

NOW 2000's
MODERN
SOAP
SINK

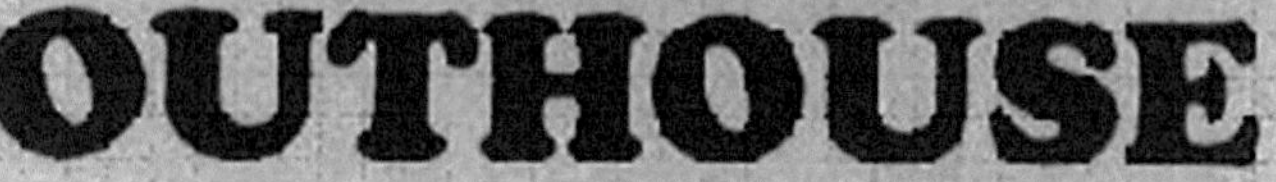

OUTHOUSE

TOILET

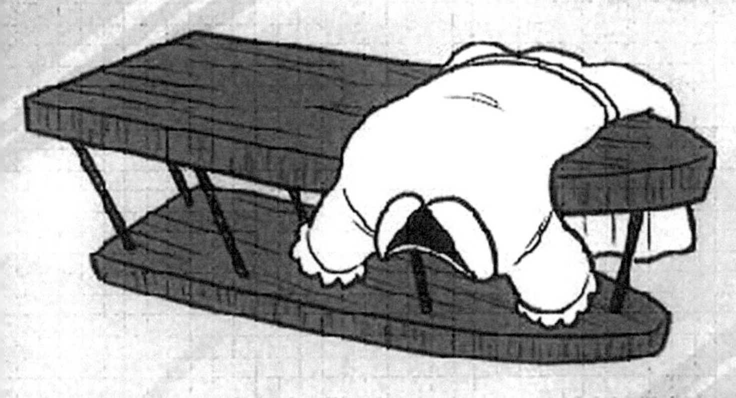

THEN 1960's
VINTAGE
WOODEN BOARD

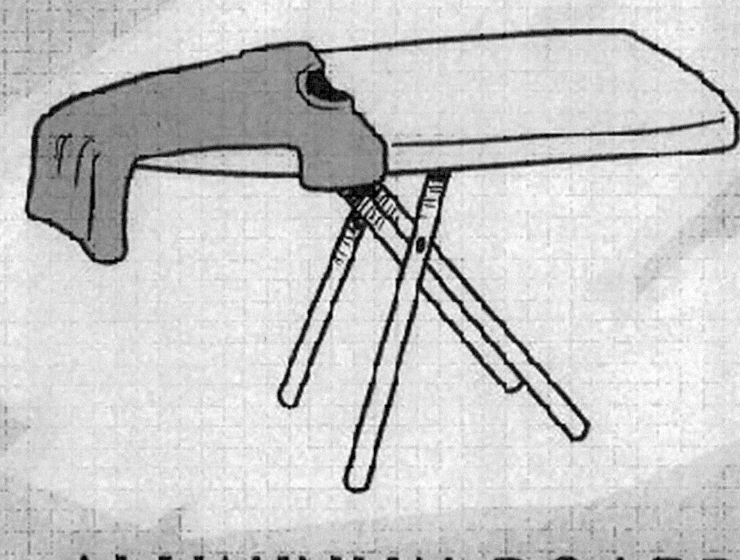

NOW 2000's
MODERN
ALUMINUM BOARD

HANDHELD IRON

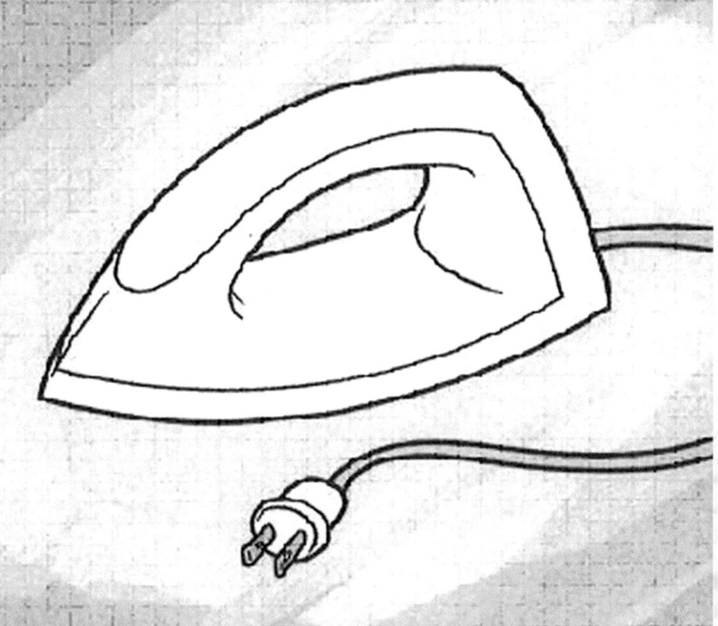

ELECTRIC IRON

THEN 1960's VINTAGE
ROLLAWAY BED

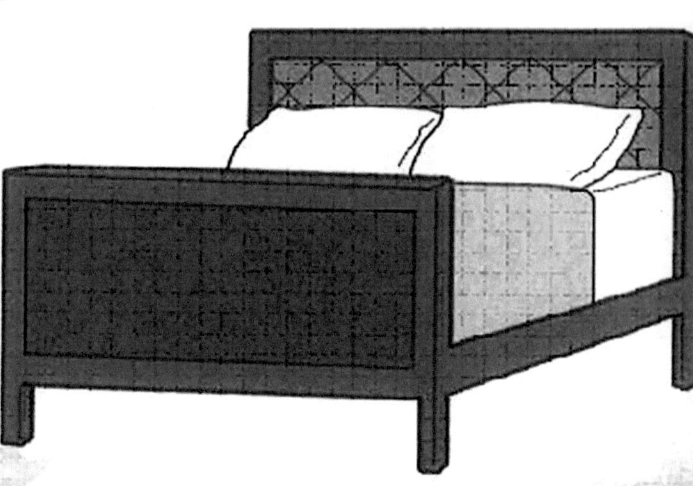

NOW 2000's MODERN
CUSTOMIZED BED

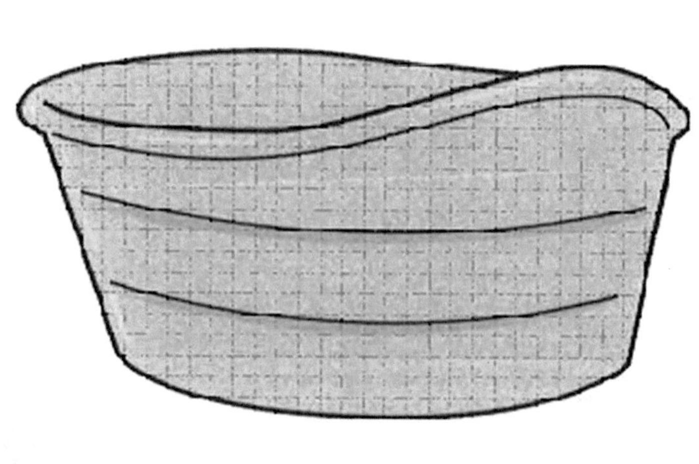

WASH TUB

BATH TUB

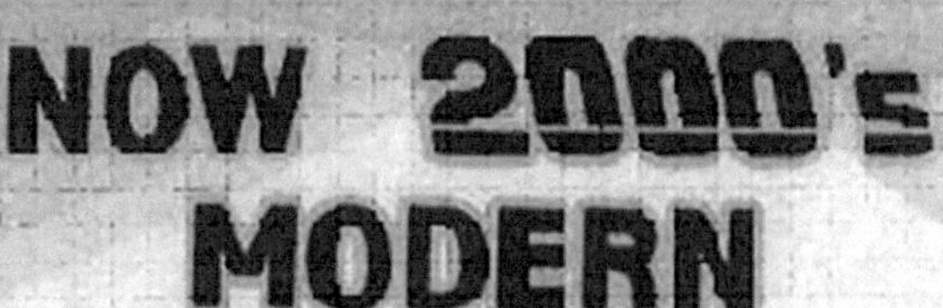

THEN 1960's VINTAGE

WOOD BURNING RANGE

NOW 2000's MODERN
ELECTRIC RANGE

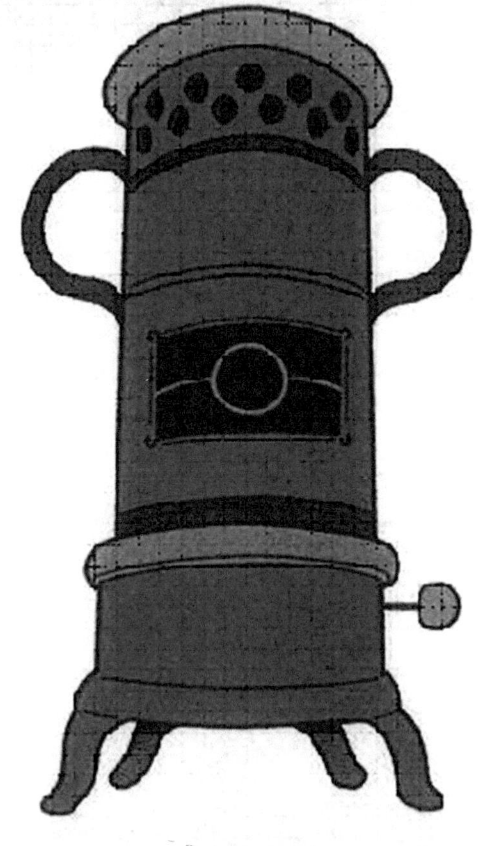

COAL FURNACE

AC UNIT

ROTARY PHONE

CELL PHONE

WASH BASIN

SINK

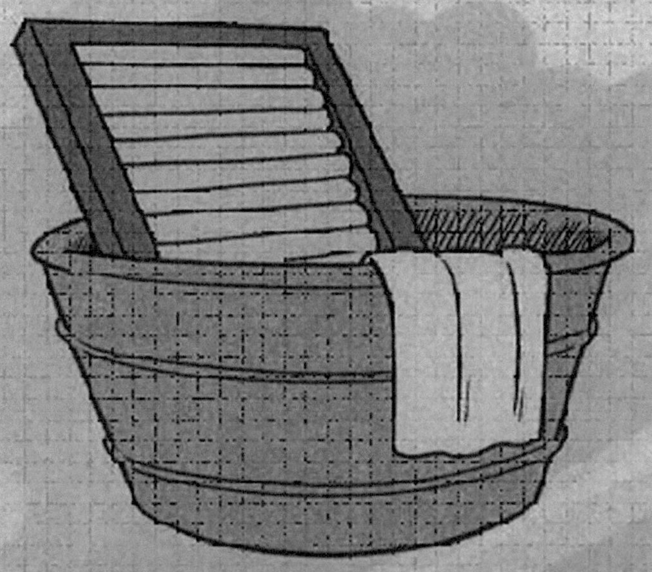

THEN 1960's VINTAGE
WASHBOARD

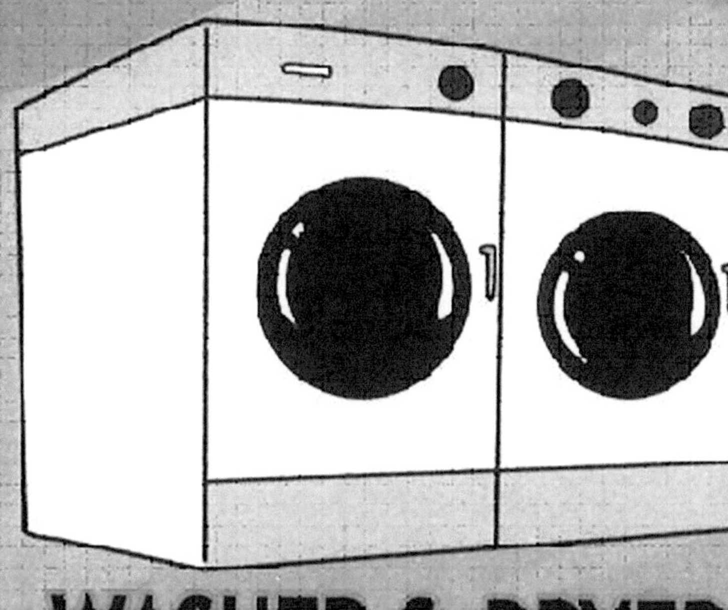

NOW 2000's MODERN
WASHER & DRYER

Old Ford Sedan

LEXUS

VOCABULARY

1.) **JIM CROW LAWS** - State and local laws enforcing racial segregation in the Southern United States. Enacted after the Reconstruction period, these laws continued in force until 1965.

2.) **POST RECONSTRUCTION** - During the early 1900's the sharecropping system had replaced slave -filled plantations as the driving force behind the Southern economy. In exchange for the use of the land, shelter and farming equipment, these laborers known as sharecroppers would give the landowner up to half of their crop yield. The system ensured that the sharecropper could never raise enough money to gain real independence.

3.) **OUTHOUSE** - A building separate from the main house with no plumbing. A place where users go to defecate or urine. Lime was used to reduce outhouse orders and warding off pesky flies.

4.) **SHARECROPPER** - someone who would farm land that belonged to a landowner. The sharecropping family would plow, plant, weed and harvest the land. However, they would only keep a small share of the crop, while the landowner would get the rest.

"If we stand tall, it is because we stand on the shoulders of our ancestors."

(African Proverb)

"A tree without roots cannot stand."

(African Proverb)

"There is a great distance between SAID and DONE."

(Puerto Rican Proverb)

"Teachers open the door, but you must enter by yourself."

(Chinese Proverb)

"To whom much is given, much is required."

(African Proverb)

"Uncommon Results requires Uncommon Measures."

Printed by Libri Plureos GmbH in Hamburg,
Germany